GUT

Miller Williams Poetry Series
EDITED BY PATRICIA SMITH

GUT

POEMS

J. Bailey Hutchinson

The University of Arkansas Press
Fayetteville | 2022

ISBN: 978-1-68226-202-3
eISBN: 978-1-61075-771-3

26 25 24 23 22   5 4 3 2 1

Manufactured in the United States of America

Designed by Liz Lester

∞ The paper used in this publication meets the minimum requirements
of the American National Standard for Permanence of Paper for
Printed Library Materials Z39.48-1984.

Library of Congress Cataloging-in-Publication Data

Names: Hutchinson, J. Bailey, author.
Title: Gut: poems / J. Bailey Hutchinson.
Description: Fayetteville: The University of Arkansas Press, 2022. |
Series: Miller Williams poetry series | Summary: "In Gut—winner of
   the first Miller Williams Poetry Prize selected by Patricia Smith—
   poet J. Bailey Hutchinson explores the substance of personal history"
   —Provided by publisher.
Identifiers: LCCN 2021047925 (print) | LCCN 2021047926
   (ebook) | ISBN 9781682262023 (paperback; alk. paper) |
   ISBN 9781610757713 (ebook)
Subjects: LCGFT: Poetry.
Classification: LCC PS3608.U85946 G88 2022 (print) | LCC
   PS3608.U85946 (ebook) | DDC 811/.6—dc23/eng/20211001
LC record available at https://lccn.loc.gov/2021047925
LC ebook record available at https://lccn.loc.gov/2021047926

for family

. . . oh clumsy, oh bumblefucked
oh giddy, oh dumbstruck . . .

—Ross Gay

CONTENTS

SERIES EDITOR'S PREFACE

I believe that all of us, every poet everywhere, can point to one mortifying moment of clueless ambition, when we decided that it was a snazzy idea to skip several thousand steps in our poetic evolution. After all, we were the annoying kids who bragged that we could and would memorize the entire dictionary, one page a day. (I threw in the towel at *abattoir*. You?)

Undeterred by the failure to master the all of our language, I once again succumbed to an unbridled zeal. Once I chose poetry as my way to walk through the world, and anxious to get down to business, I decided that I'd teach myself prosody and form in one big ol' fell swoop. Who needed classrooms and seminars and actual instruction? I'd picked up the enticing tome *Patterns of Poetry*, by some guy named Miller Williams, in the best lil' bookstore in Chicago, and I'd set aside a whole month to memorize everything in its pages.

Imagine—an entire *month* to master iambs, dactyls, anapests, pyrrhus, spondees, trochees and amphibrachs, as well as sapphics, the elegiac couplet, englyn penfyr, dipodic quatrain, awdyl gywydd, clerihew, terza rima, cyhydedd hir, rhupunt, and—well, the sonnet, of course.

This Williams person, whoever he was (remember that I was—shall we say, oblivious to everything except my own naked desire to POET), had gathered all that juicy knowledge between two covers, and all I had to do was sit down and pick it up. I imagined him on a misty mountainside somewhere, wallowing in wisdom and doling out prosody. I'd soon be joining him.

Needless to say, failure was my one and only option. It is notoriously difficult to teach yourself metrics because so much depends on hearing it from someone who's got it mastered and internalized. As Annie Finch—the woman who eventually got poetic rhythms through my thick skull—said, "If you never feel it in your body, you'll never feel it."

It is also notoriously difficult to teach the emotional and narrative nuances of form. A poet has a dizzying amount of power when it comes to topic, perspective, and voice, and even more power when it comes to choosing the form that will pull it all together. As I like to tell my students, every single choice you make as a poet instructs the reader in the reading of the poem. EVERY. SINGLE. CHOICE.

In the midst of tackling *Patterns of Poetry* and failing miserably at both the patterns and the poetry, I thought I'd take some time to get to know more about that Williams fella. Whenever he used his own poems as examples in the book, I was tempted to throw the volume across the room into the nearest wall—they were that good.

I still crave the gorgeously stuttered music of the elegiac couplets in "For Victor Jara":

> This is to say we remember. Not that remembering saves us.
> Not that remembering brings anything usable back.
>
> This is to say that we never have understood how to say this.
> Out of our long unbelief what do we say to belief?

And this, my favorite excerpt from "On the Way Home from Nowhere, New Year's Eve":

> I tell myself I am blind. In such a dark
> I could be moving down the spaceless form
> of time, a painted tunnel. I twist off
> my shoes and walk in darkness. Leap.

Soon I realized that the idea of book learnin' myself into poetic prowess was a hopeless undertaking. But instead of giving up altogether, I decided to do a deep dive into Mr. Williams's work. I learned for the first time that he'd been William Jefferson Clinton's inaugural poet ("Whose law was never so much of the hand as the head / cannot let chaos make its way to the heart . . ."). I scoured the *Poetry* magazine archives, where this stanza of "For Rebecca, for Whom Nothing Has Been Written Page after Page" waited for me:

> When all the words are written down and read
> and even the creeping weights are written in
> what matters is what remains not said, not said.
> Which is what long silences are for.

And in his book *The Ways We Touch*, I found the wee treasure "Compassion," which urges its reader to shower each and everyone with empathy "even if they don't want it"—because—

> You do not know what wars are going on
> down there where the spirit meets the bone.

Well, amen.

After throwing his books against the wall in frustration, what drew me deeper into Miller Williams's work? The same thing that should draw me to yours.

I look for new ways to look at things I've already seen—things I'm convinced I know. I look for a hook for my breath to catch on. I look for form—traditional that enhances, instead of suffocates, its subject matter. Williams makes me jealous. He makes me wish I'd written it first.

And according to the man himself: "One of the best things that has ever been said about my work was said by a critic who wrote that 'Miller Williams is the Hank Williams of American poetry. While his poetry is taught at Princeton and Harvard, it's read and understood by squirrel hunters and taxi drivers.'"

In other words, I'm addicted to poetry that knows no closed doors.

It's been years between the time I first reveled in the words of this newfound poet and the day I became the editor of this series that carries his name. But both nothing much and everything has changed. I still need and expect to be knocked to the floor by a poem. I need it to hold me down, make me breathe differently. I'm a selfish reader. I want everything from a poem—and I know, for a fact, that everything isn't too much. *I want poems that vivify.*

You may, at this very moment, be thinking about submitting your lovingly spit-shined manuscript to the contest. If so, I have some pointers. (First of all, don't spit on it.)

My stellar contest screeners are also my teachers—I see in their work that they are dead set on narrative and lyrical impact, so I'm certain that the poems they read and forwarded to me have reached for that dual goal and achieved it.

But they also saw many manuscripts that weren't quite ready for the big time—by poets I like to think of as "feverishly pulling the trigger, but lacking ammunition"—or manuscripts that were enthusiastically submitted to exactly the wrong contest. The directive is, and always will be, very very simple: Read the description of what we want. Then send your one-of-a-kind, patented version of *that*.

In my college classrooms, officially "grading" poetry has always struck me as a bit of a crapshoot, because students enter at so many different levels with so many different ideas of what poetry is. I once had a fledgling writer pen a textured and lyrically complicated persona poem in the voice of a chambered bullet. In the very same class, a lovelorn student wrote, "When you left me, you hurt my emotions."

But the manuscripts that poured into the Miller Williams contest, for the most part, had obviously been sweated, prayed, and wept over, revised to pinpoint, whipped into formidable shape. There was a universal goodness to the mix, even if not everyone paid close enough attention to the type of work requested. But, oh—the top three certainly did. Each, in their own way, rocked the rafters.

Once J. Bailey Hutchinson's *Gut* rocketed to the top of the pile, it pretty much stayed there. Yes, there were contenders who threatened the throne, but *Gut* was always strolling in the neighborhood of the kingdom. It's startling and innovative and—how shall I say this?—a little bit of everyone. You'll see yourself here somewhere.

I really wish I'd written it.

But making sure it reaches you is definitely the next best thing.

Listen to this. It's the closing lines of "Ouroboros as Eight-Year-Old," one of the poems in the book about Bailey growing up with ADHD:

> she leans down to kiss the top of my head and I leap, I put her teeth through her lip. And. She holds. My mother's arms come around me. Even as I boil. Even as I pulse. Even as *spilled swim-bladder which is accumulated dollop of sap which is liquid which sticks which is inside an eel-bird inside a gas giant* which is blood on my scalp, which is my mother's exploded mouth, teeth two pearls in a red bed, *which is deconstructed willow-weeper which is a nest of purpled popsicle sticks,* she holds. Even as I become a jar of furious bones. She holds. My head a walnut in the quiet vise of her chin. Swollen grape in a lionsmouth.

There you have it. One of the many hooks I caught my breath on. The sound. The surprise. The collision of phrases I thought could never collide. The current of love and trust flowing beneath it all.

What stands out about Bailey's work is her singular voice, graced with the ease and imagination of a born storyteller. She's a southern girl who sees no need to pound in that fact with a narrative hammer. She simply lifts you up and places you in the dead center of an addictive poetic lifeline, populated by cinema-worthy backdrops and people who refuse to stop nudging once you're done with the book.

The unforgiving edges of the poet's grandmother, Barbara, that "mean / sleepwalking woman" whose ghost "comes up from the river, drenched in coontail kelp and fresh-mussel, // pale   as a goat throat."

Bailey's mother Mitzi, she of the wise and halting wisdoms, steps alive in the multisectioned "Became My Body, Too," stanzas of fractured and loving lineage. Here, a young Mitzi watches for her sister's seizures.

> At night, Mitzi would kneel by her sister's bunk
> with a garden-trowel   the grip all gnawed,
> (*how can a mouth   so small   blister*
>   *beechwood?*)—watching
> for the pulse of jaw,   the frenetic socket-whirl
> that took the girl's body
> before she became crack of cymbal   and seafloor lightning.

And her granddaddy Hoyle—his ways with women and meat, his hard ways of loving—will be with you for a long, long time. This, from "The Butcher's Granddaughter":

> This body. Its rope. Before some pea-ball burst
> his brain, I remember Hoyle's belly—me, curled
> like a grub there, grogged on applesauce. He smelled
> like a good lunch meat, the biggest man I knew, singing
> *too-ra-loo-ra-lai* through a mouth I never heard bite.

In addition, Bailey has mastered something I look for that not many poets can accomplish, something I'm constantly trying to get better at—when there's something she wants the reader to feel and there's no exact word for it, she conjures a phrase: Beer "nickeling

my brain's-edge." A man is "shirt-wrecked by a midnight nosebleed."
"Screwed to a scaffold, body-water glossy, / the hog opens like a Bible."
A postcard is crammed with "cricket-leg lettering."

J. Bailey Hutchinson keeps introducing me and introducing me
and introducing me to more and more brand-new world. Nothing set-
tles. Nothing sits still. Nothing "makes do."

Thanks to this utterly original voice, my very first series pick is
everything I was looking for.

Meanwhile, Janet Jackson (how's that for a segue?), who I go to for
all my pithy wisdom, once said of her famously gruff father, "My dad
taught us that there's no greater distance than that between first and
second place."

That most definitely applies if you're a Jackson, but not in the case
of Casey Thayer and his amazing second-place manuscript *Rational
Anthem*.

It's hard to find a way to say this without someone taking offense,
but *Rational Anthem* is a stellar *boy* book, pulsing with the triumphs
and downfalls of testosterone, a muscled book, a book that's decidedly
cocked and loaded. It's a book of men who drag their feet through vio-
lence. It's a painstakingly scrawled love letter to firepower. It chronicles
men in their struggles with tenderness and vulnerability. It's the hunter
and the blood and gristle the hunter knows. It's a book that not many
people—certainly not many men, tangled in the roots of everything
they think they should be—could write with such revelation and
nuance.

Consider this, from "An Anatomical Study Concerning the North
American Whitetail":

> You can love a man and find some shared action
> in which he tolerates that love.
>
> I slid my hands up the hollow muffler
> of the buck's chest cavity
>
> and slit the esophagus, cut the skirt
> of the diaphragm from sternum to crotch.
>
> Then I pulled the guts out. Sometimes
> I believe in small acts of kindness.

Rational Anthem often finds itself at the juncture of what a man does and what he dares to feel, and for the reader that's traditionally a shadowy and unknowable place. But Casey fearlessly inhabits that space, moving in the lens until we move from discomfort to discovery:

> **bullet ✦ 1.** what thunder, teeth / in the threat, / blade in the sheath, / blood-letter bought / over the counter as easy as aspirin or an Oxy / to take into the body, / what the deed / leaves, hand that reaches / across the field, / snake coiled in the warren, / mole mazing the loam, / what the body carries, what is left / of the deed . . .

I certainly don't mean to imply that *Rational Anthem* is *all* boy. There is much notable otherwise in its pages, including an unsettling ars poetica, an unstructured abecedarian that hits like a backhand slap, and cameos by Aquaman and an adopted blue whale.

But what *Rational Anthem* offers is crucial insight on how men think when they can't help but think. As the opening stanza of "The next great American elegy in the effigy of" indicates, the book is a deep dive into that riddle:

> you, who bonged from a severed boar's head
> Yuengling poured down its throat into your throat,
> who let the jaws of that giant clamp yours in a kiss,
> you, feral and triumphant in owning an animal for sport.

Casey Thayer's fearless exploration of masculinity is nothing less than revelatory. It manages to be contemplative and insightful, while packing a relentless punch. I will surely be gifting it to a few manly types who I hope will benefit from its bravery.

Since Janet Jackson never blurted any wisdoms about *third* place (my guess is that, for her father, no such thing existed), I won't be quoting her again in my introduction of Michael Mlekoday's *All Earthly Bodies*.

While Bailey and Casey do their vivifying head-on, with narratives that unfurl like cinema, Michael's punch is quieter—but its more gradual force, wrapped in a muscled language, still whips your head around. I loud-whispered "damn!" so often while reading this manuscript, my husband—the crime-writing poetry snob—barged into my office to see what was doing such a number on my head.

So I read him the opening lines of "Revolting":

Even the gaze
is a kind of government

and even the outlaw
wants sometimes
to kneel

if only in a field
as full as a revolver.

And, just like that, he understood.

After the names of the winner and runners-up were initially revealed, I looked into their backgrounds. I was surprised and delighted to discover that Michael had been a regular participant in the poetry slam, the often-controversial competition where head-on vivifying is pretty much the order of the day.

The slam, aside from being a sometimes-chaotic performative arena, was also an invaluable training ground for the development of physical and social witnessing that brought *All Earthly Bodies* to this moment. In a perfect world, this is what the slammer becomes—a poet at the crosswords of resistance and rhythm, someone who knows that poetry's power resides not only in the scream, but often in the whisper.

Listen to this excerpt from the heart-numbing "The Night the Murderous Cop Was Not Charged":

I want to know where
all this weeping and standing
has taken us, exactly. [...]

Does the infinite static
of the Pacific's evening tide—
everbearing, acidifying—
flicker itself to justice?

Can the long memories
of the pines imagine
something like restitution
for all the blades, blights,

and wildfires we call
history?

And it is Michael who penned that snippet I printed out and pinned above my desk. There's always that passage that steps gingerly from the manuscript to shake you into a new awake. Here it is, from "Whites":

But what is quotation exactly,
if not a way to wield another's prayer
and pretend it is not our own.

What language is not borrowed
machinery, echo of another's ancestors
burrowing the whole field of you,

blooming a grain you can't name
but harvest regardless.

—*Patricia Smith*

ACKNOWLEDGMENTS

Thank you to the following journals for homing my poems, sometimes as earlier versions: *Bear Review*: "Self-Portrait as Haruno Sakura, Kunoichi of Konohagakure"; *Beloit Poetry Journal*: "I Have Never Had to Love Someone Who Beat Me," "Real Good Meat Eater," "Things Dying & Where [It seems my father has been old]," and "The Minnesota State Fair's Miracle of Birth Center, Sponsored by Subaru"; *BOAAT* journal: "Poem Written as Barter for $366.12 in Outstanding Bills"; *The Boiler* journal: "J. Bailey Hutchinson Takes Plan B in Marseille" and "Fox Song"; *FreezeRay*: "Self-Portrait as Tomoe Mami, Beheaded by a Witch"; *Lit*: "Things Dying & Where [A feral kitten is a big-eyed thing]"; *Muzzle* magazine: "Lineage"; *New South*: "Carne e Spirito"; *Nimrod International Journal of Prose and Poetry*: "Became My Body, Too"; *Ninth Letter*: "Eat"; *Peach Mag*: "Butterflies Are More Metal than Moths" and "J. Bailey Hutchinson Moves 658.8 Miles North and Tries to Make It Count"; *Salamander*: "Learning to Swim in the Mississippi"; *Wyvern Lit*: "Ouroboros as Eight-Year-Old," "Dog Not Deer," "Things Dying & Where [M says the neighbor's house is burning and I]," and "J. Bailey Hutchinson Prays to the River."

I am indescribably grateful to the dazzling Patricia Smith for selecting *Gut* as the winner of the 2022 Miller Williams Prize. Thank you for your enthusiasm, your editorial acuity, and your faith in my work. I'm sorry I didn't pick up the phone the first time you called.

Thank you to the team at the University of Arkansas Press for making this book a physical thing—a thing of beauty, a decades-long dream made tangible. I still can't believe it. And thank you, Anthony Blake, for the *perfect* book cover.

For inspiration, for guidance, for mentorship, for community: thank you to my MFA cohort and friends in Fayetteville, especially Geffrey Davis, Molly Bess Rector, Jacob Lindberg, Zachary Harrod, Peter Mason, Gwen Mauroner, Toni Jensen, MaryKate Messimer, Brandon Weston, Alys Dutton, Elizabeth DeMeo, Davis McCombs, Geoff Brock, Padma Viswanathan, and Jane Blunschi. Thank you also to Marlin M. Jenkins, Aeon Ginsberg, Caki Wilkinson, and Ashley

Roach-Freeman, beloved friends and readers. I owe the work to you; I owe the joy found alongside the work to you; I owe my faith in poetry to you; I owe so much, and to many others not named here.

I am so grateful for the time and breathing room provided by the following literary organizations and institutions, where many of these poems first blossomed: the University of Arkansas MFA Program in Creative Writing and Translation, the Community of Writers Poetry Workshop, the Sewanee Writers' Conference, Sundress Academy for the Arts—and to the most tenderly held of all, the Open Mouth Literary Center. Thank you to the writers I met in these and other writing spaces; you are, to my immense good fortune, too numerous to name. As I write this I see each of your faces in my mind, smiling, luminous. I will thank all of you in person one day.

Thank you to my family: my mother, Mitzi, my lodestone, who is a presence in this manuscript both literal and figurative; to my father, Steve, and stepmother, Audrey, for relentlessly cheering me on; to my uncle Richard, fellow citizen of the booklover nation; to my brother, Brandon, for hearing me always, my sister-in-law, Lining, stronger than all of us, and my niece, Vivian, simply for being; and to my late step-father and late grandmother, gone before I could celebrate this book with them. No one owns a story—we share them, and I am grateful to share so many with you all.

And thanks also to my friends, many of whom watched me bloom from a small nerd scribbling in a journal during algebra class to a big nerd doing roughly the same thing. Thank you especially John Partain, Rose Baker, India Acklin, Ben Williamson, and Kaleb Yaniger.

Ah, I could go on. I love you. I love you. I love you.

GUT

Things Dying & Where

A feral kitten is a big-eyed thing. Bald & suspicious. Too quick for
the rude bumble of me, squatted by the crawl space. From here grew a
smell, creaks of many little hungers. Whispers or feet. Sometimes the
grown cats' woven yowling. If I woke early enough I'd see them—big
or blue & dusted—returning to the house with limp dinners. Low-
slung bellies. *They sleep*, my mother told me, can-opening, *all day,
and hunt all night, to feed their babies.* More than I feared the dark &
underwater sounds I wanted to touch a mean little body. Shallow a
pinky in its ear. So. I'd wait at the mouth of this place, catching sight
of a taut head, flits of paw.

But one day something grey & small as a tongue waited, sleeping!
Lucky! by the dark opening, and—I noticed suddenly its eyes semi-
open, packed with a translucent gunk. The secret black line of its lips
dry and tight against teeth. I knew. I knew I didn't want to die. But I
was six & alone on a big, big farm so I touched it with one finger then
two. Then with my whole hand, felt the sharp structure of rib. My
shadow covered this body like a swaddling and I held it, put it against
the flat of my chest, touched its awful tail. I didn't know how sad to
be. Then I heard the sneeze-like yank of a parking brake, my mother
suddenly present, saying *honey no, no, put that down.* I said *okay,* and
I know.

J. Bailey Hutchinson Prays to the River

after Heather Dobbins & Christian Anton Gerard

and make me tall, Miss, so I may locate casserole dishes.

govern my water consumption in reasonable

cranks, turn leek-long the grass to bury my doorframe

in sucked-onion-scent. you've drunk a lot of bodies, Miss, while

everyone stood and looked—even me, though I am ready

to sift silt, panning teeth and bones—but, Miss, while I work,

tighten your hold on my grandmother Barbara

who visits my windowsill in many shapes (luminous beetle,

cat with active glands, wine). I am afraid of her. and Miss,

drown the heart that quickens at a good glance,

at a long sigh, at a slice of summer squash left

on his plate. drown the heart that quickens when he loves me.

drown the heart that quickens his quickening

then frights dry as opened gourd. Miss, I know I can die

alone, Miss, because I've come this far, crushed every

fiddleback I've found though I know

they lived here first, but Miss, I fear the soup they make

of a lonely knee so it's me (purpling worker, thick

with liquid) or them (solidified nightmare claw),

so Miss, make me more endurant in thirst,

and if that means you shape my limbs,

bend back the joint, taper muscle-and-meat ticker-

tape thin, all swaddled in dun-fur, I'll reckon it a blessing.

be newly coyoted—Miss, banish the house-shapes:

curt pile of mouse shit, ghost of my grandmother?

bone-knife rusting in my sink, ghost of a man's desire?

shatter of moonlit rosemary, ghost of a thousand spiders? and still

the onions, I underestimated, it's probably

an unreasonable amount of onions, plus I

don't want to give Barbara—dog-jawed and dimpled

with moonlight—a new place to hide. Miss, for this, I offer

the longest of my birthdays. the purple I tend.

and Miss, I offer the garden,

I offer an opal boiled in the stomach

of a rabbit and sealed with fat-cap, if,

Miss, you'll only make me tall.

Heat Advisory

*The city opens cooling centers when the heat index is at least
105 degrees for more than three hours per day for two days in
a row, or if the heat index is more than 115 degrees at any time.*

—WREG News

Summer in Memphis—my body thick-
coated in oil, bark musk,

greased to my mother's lawn chair—
I have: no shirt. No hat.

Jean shorts & a bowl
of frozen sugar peas. Or—

melting sugar peas. I sheathe
each pea between my lip & gum;

once they hit a tooth's
temperature, they get licked

into the yard. *Wasteful,*
my mother mouths through the window

of her fan-drenched
bedroom. *Planting peas,*

I tell her. On days like this
she can't go outside—air

slurried with pollen & earth's
wet groan, the bald sky

holding the sun like a rag
to her mouth. At fourteen,

my mother told me, she
broke a girl's arm with a board

in the only air-conditioned room
in Whitehaven—I imagine her, first,

browsing fenceposts, following
this girl to the community center,

pausing at the double doors
to say *I'm sorry I*

have to hurt ya. Now, at the window,
again my mother mouths—

something illegible
through heat-shimmer. Maybe

quit suckin those peas. Maybe
don't make me come out there.

Heat makes mean,
like a little girl

with a beating board.
Like the hot night

my eardrum burst & I
screamed myself a sweat-stain,

my head a wailing redbean
in my mother's lap.

Now, at the window, she
watches me not-hear her.

I press my leg, spangle
the skin white-through-red,

marveling my cooked flank.
My whole bones.

Learning to Swim in the Mississippi

I. Origins

What Jubilee saw at Putt-Putt Camp
wadint no tire swing. Spanned maybe

a whole meander-or-two, crooked.
Heard it can bloom up big enough to

buck the Hernando, or shrink around
a baby's-ankle; some call it cooking names

like Boil. Or Pickle. *Jubilee called it*
Meemaw. Thing about a wyrm is

they never nice and got no wings
nor legs to bring the mean elsewhere,

cruel as a booker's wallet or pulling berries
before they color, so—in the deep dark down

of the river (two hundred feet in April)
you have: catfish big as a dugong,

boat hides, beer bottles, bones of folks
who thought *well a river won't*

riptide, and the holy wrought groove
of the Delta Wyrm. Wild kinda spook,

isn't it? You try and poison a snake
she'll come up on your porch,

slide the whole cola-pot down her throat.
A thousand or just two teeth.

II. Parlay

One day, river-stinking like a sucked-on bib, I stumped on a water
moccasin—but before it bit, the water's edge moved, sucking it back
into—what? Mud? The murky yawn of something bigger? I couldn't
suss it; I thought it looked like a cartoon; a question mark popping
out of a shoe. I chewed my cheek. That night I went to bed expecting
hot sleep, but instead got took by a dream, sudden and heavy back
to the river. Waist-deep I started—then, nearby, a mound gathered.
Blister. Bubble. I shied like a dog. When it ruptured and a bright heat
washed down my stuck thumb of a body, what came up was a catfish
big as a house, barbels shivering. I remembered—the snake, that
horrible hungry mudmouth—and the big-bodied thing slunk closer.
I said hello. I said my name. It opened its mouth, mud-scent shoaling
my nose.

III. Inheritance

For eight months, I live with my grandmother
while learning what kind of woman I want to be.

I feast on dark beer, boiled coffee, a hive
of jams (blackberry thick as ichor, muddy-bread,

apple butter). I often wake to her howling, thinking
there is a man in here I must kill, but each time I only

find her asleep thumbsdeep in solitaire, a novel in her lap
(and some ranch hand's greased-up chest spread there).

Still, I let myself be summoned by this urgent woah (beer
still nickeling my brain's-edge). I go to her, gape-mawed

on the couch, ninety-four years of dreams tissuing her face.
One night, I wait for it, mapping her dream, its yelp-and-gargle.

Leaning in, I search the gradual trap of her mouth, sloe dark,
for—I don't know what, a coal, a thorn. Something I can

take out of her. But I'm nervous of the unnamed, and when I ask
the next day, *what do you always dream of,* she says

simple things.   *Dark. Doors. Mud. Water.*

Big Dark

New moon tonight
you yodel, each

ruddied knee crest-
ing the hammock.

Dusk suckers
the space between trees.

A butterfly nurses
your baseball cap.

I have
a ritual.

Though all day
we have just drunk

beer and wasted
kindling, I am tired.

I am no one's
ideal outdoorsman—

grousing about tick
risks, the stark

stillness of air
in a tent.

We write intentions
on a square of paper;

I write the words
no fears no fears

no fears no fears
in the lessening

light, & later,
when you lead me

lampless from
the clearing

to burn my paper
to the pinch-bit,

I do not
let the match

snuff. I wonder
how you know

a place without
its moon. When I

was young,
a thunderstorm

rattled me
awake—the dark

a witch in my bed,
a body double, her

gym-whistle wail
& nightbawl

cold breath
on my face.

I answered
in a language

boiled up
from my most

wickedest organs,
blood quick-thickening

behind my eyes
until a vessel burst.

Now, crawling
back to camp, I cast

my flashlight's frantic
eye on each root

& edge—despite
your elbow

in my grip. Night
is a fabric of black

chicken-scent.
Some bugs' eyes

get big enough
to shine back.

Ouroboros as Eight-Year-Old

*For all good poetry is the spontaneous overflow of powerful feelings:
and though this be true, Poems to which any value can be attached
were never produced on any variety of subjects but by a man who,
being possessed of more than usual organic sensibility, had also
thought long and deeply.*

—William Wordsworth, *Preface to Lyrical Ballads*

Standing with my mother beside the bumper boats at Bogey's
Celebration Station and Mini Golf, a woman asks my name and I
say *coal-fattened serpent which is a lit and vibrating thing which is a
fish-school frantic and rubied which is circles and circles and circles*, and I,
brimming, near bite through each cheek, I say *opening spiderlily which
is a fractal of tongues which is a thousand yellow-birds which is a bat-
bulked steeple which is an eel*, some engine moltening in me, my right
palm *cat's-eye supergiant* my left palm *shuddering barrel of quartz*,

and when the doctor pinched coin after coin of blood from the tip
of my finger *which is a screaming carrot on fire*, she said well isn't this a
little squaller while I slicked my mother's hands with all of my body's
musterable liquids and my mother said baby sit still *which is a badger
chewing matchsticks which is a stovetop which is a carpet of nightsoil and
cave-cricket*, and the doctor said well isn't this a proper thunderhead,
does she sleep through the night, does she ever sit still, and my
mother said baby sit still,

and in the line for bumper boats my mother says my name and
leans down and I leap, she leans down to my head and I leap, she
leans down to kiss the top of my head and I leap, I put her teeth
through her lip. And. She holds. My mother's arms come around
me. Even as I boil. Even as I pulse. Even as *spilled swim-bladder which
is accumulated dollop of sap which is liquid which sticks which is inside
an eel-bird inside a gas giant* which is blood on my scalp, which is
my mother's exploded mouth, teeth two pearls in a red bed, *which is
deconstructed willow-weeper which is a nest of purpled popsicle sticks*, she
holds. Even as I become a jar of furious bones. She holds. My head a
walnut in the quiet vise of her chin. Swollen grape in a lionsmouth.

Self-Portrait as Tomoe Mami, Beheaded by a Witch

Given ribbon, I make musket.
And this is no easy thing to build:

the ramrod, breech, the powder-filled
bladder, channels of oil and flint.

All this mustered with folded legs
and jaw-grit before dinner, meeting

my own eye in the mirror. Sulfur or opal.
Mortar or knee-sock. How to be a girl

and also bury bullets: sign a contract.
I wonder what a witch is, if she

has a saucer for her tea. With sugar.
Jarred honeycomb. I didn't know

my name-on-the-line meant
the kind of forever that gathers

for pickling each major vessel, organ.
Heats each leg's nervous gristle

so, even in death, I stand rifle-cocked.
God of this body, you gave me

ribbon, though I asked for *please, an ungiving*
thing. So I can find others in the dark.

So I can clock a beast in the eye.

Eat

Once, I watched
a tall, pale man
stoke a fire, remove
his flannel
to keep it—I guess—
from the flames' big licks,
and as his skin grew
more luminous,
the subglacial
strum-and-yield
of a slight canvas,
I kept thinking:
how much
does he eat?
Could I eat
more than him?
I bet
I could eat
more than him.
I mean,
one time
I ordered thirteen Krystals
with cheese, I assured
the fearful woman
at the register,
and fries.
A Krystal burger's
no bigger
than a fist,

the buns like
half a damp Kleenex,
the patty (*rat
burger*, my father
teased) soused
in mustard,
burying
whatever might
cling to beef
that boiled.
I ate them all.
Did not fall sick.
My stomach is
thirteen fists.
Do you know
what I mean
when I say
I have types
of hunger? Like
the twenty years
I didn't let my-
self cry, then
I did—I mean,
I really cried,
round and taut
as a frog's
vocal sac—
I couldn't
stop, weeping
in a truck-

bed, in the Arcade,
in a guestroom.
Weeping in Terminal C,
in the ocean naked,
in Sweden. Weeping
in the black beans,
which I routinely
underseason.
I am always
scheming
the next mess
and who'll
watch me
eat it. Once,
I took a friend
from Wisconsin (a man
so kind and hungry
he thickens his
mac-n-cheese
until it catches
the spoon)
to a catfish buffet
in Searcy.
I didn't say it,
but I was eyeing
the hushpuppy hoards,
filets cocooned
in cornmeal, hock-speckled
beans, pudding.
Him greening

three plates in.
Me licking gravy
from my arm.
Do you know
what I mean
when I say
eating, sometimes,
has nothing to do
with hunger?
You are
the eatingest
girl,
my father said.
I love
how little
you are,
said a bad
date. I can't
do a pushup
but I will
sweep six plates.
Do you know
what I mean
when I say my eating
spooks? To the root?
Every man.
The cream
and greens
body of me.

The Minnesota State Fair's Miracle of Birth Center, Sponsored by Subaru

Before I smell it, I imagine
I smell it: copper-slick, torn.
Butter and musk. What gathers

in a working groin. The barn's
no different than outside, really—
foot-beaten and humid, maybe

a little more soiled—and inside, a cow
heaves curtains of red tissue
from her backside. Quilt of trembling

oil. *Oh, that's just afterbirth*, the vet
tells me. The cow's bored eyewhite
stark in her skull. Her chin fretted gossamer.

Nearby, a bursting rabbit endures waves
of toddler-palm; if you're gentle, you get
a blue ribbon (*First Place in Not Hurting*

Something Smaller than You), and I think:
everything parts for children. Crowds. Knees.
Thin velvet of a lambscheek, for which

my hand also hungers—to touch
what is new and milk-drunk. To cup
something pink and cropped, mysteriously

focal. A sign on the wall lists the times
of each new birth: 6:14 AM, three lambs—
Becky, Delilah, Marge—that I can't see

through the kneeling team of boys
by the pen, their lager-yellow
crew cuts. Only the mother sheep, who

looms to the left. Her indecipherable eye
between bars.

J. Bailey Hutchinson Takes Plan B in Marseille

One of last night's dark corners: J. Bailey Hutchinson palmed keys
into her roommate's pocket, in the club, the taxi—or maybe
the alley where she knocked the bark clean off her knee. *I knocked*

the bark clean off my knee, J. Bailey Hutchinson crooned into a tall
man's neck, & he held her, thumbed the run in her tights & gentled
the bruise blooming there. J. Bailey Hutchinson didn't believe herself

beautiful enough for this man who loomed her out of the bar, who said,
I will get us a hotel. Anywhere. Anywhere. Please stay, angel. Last night,
they found a room by the port & J. Bailey Hutchinson didn't know

a man's thigh could be so smooth, or how it felt to be pored-over. *You are*
my little angel, the man told J. Bailey Hutchinson, & when he slipped into
another language she read his body: blushing neck & *darling*, hair slick

to the root & *lovely*, tightly angled waist & *want*. Now, leaning against
her sorbet-orange door, sea-air & sleep-grease slick on her scalp,
J. Bailey Hutchinson has ten euros & an Amex. No keys. Now,

J. Bailey Hutchinson has to ask a neighbor *où est la pharmacie?* & he points her
towards a green neon cross, squat and lineated. Inside, J. Bailey Hutchinson
approaches the counter, wipes her upper lip. *S'il vous plaît*, she says, low,

shame a hairless foot on her chest. In her mouth. *Je voudrais Plan B.*
She says *bee*, not *beh*, & wonders if the woman behind the counter has a daughter
old enough to let a man lug her into the shower. *Huit euros*, the woman says, but

J. Bailey Hutchinson doesn't move because she is convinced this
is supposed to be difficult, so the woman repeats, *ate urr-os, please.*
Mer, says J. Bailey Hutchinson. *Merci beaucoup.* Later, J. Bailey Hutchinson

will receive a postcard fat with stamps & cricket-leg lettering. *I am telling to people
how I was kind of in love with the American that I pass a amazing and magical night
and day.* Today, J. Bailey Hutchinson uses her last two euros to buy a coffee

& undresses the blister-pack. So small. No bigger than a screwhead.
J. Bailey Hutchinson places it in her mouth, deepens it into the soft
sublingual flesh of her tongue. With espresso. Swallows.

I Have Never Had to Love Someone Who Beat Me

The last time Hoyle laid hands on his daughter,
cousin Kenny was parked at the curb, crude-ing
growed up words with my thirteen-year-old mom
—meanwhile, Hoyle panthered the porch, dense
and glistening, saying *better get your ass back*
in this house fore I skin it, and when my mom
said *no*, boy did that big man move, got her arm
in his hand like a yearling, but she beat him to the belt,
snatched it clean out the loops, and he said, *little girl*
you better let that go, and when my mom said *no*,
she buckle-whipped his gut, and my mom tells me
all this like it's sweet. *Daddy wasn't being vicious*,
she says. *Kenny was a real nasty boy.* The blood
would've wrecked his shirt, if he'd been wearing one.

Obituary

Shirt-wrecked by a midnight nosebleed,
Hoyle kneels in the TV room. We are a dry-
sinused folk—known to crack in wintertime,
when the heater drinks all air worth breathing
—so it's possible he   doesn't mean to die.
That he doesn't note his puddling lips. The static
snowing his eyes. But. A lonesome stroke's
more fatal than most, and Barbara's been gone
fourteen months, so. Maybe when his knuckles
get lead-heavy, when he can't swallow the clot
gathering in his throat, when he waits a whole
two hours to call my mother, tongue-muffled,
he knows

                    exactly what it means.

Barbara

She's a mean
sleepwalking woman.
Hoyle makes two babies with her.
He finds her, sometimes,
longitudinal on the ottoman
or arm deep in pantyhose,
ghost-combing her hair
with an empty fist.
One night, Hoyle feels her
sit up in bed, touches the hip
bitten by her broad rimmed
underwear. Almost misses
what she's doing, still asleep:
loading his revolver.

The Holes

Next to his revolver, Hoyle squirrels bullets.
Every summer he pays kids too small for
Piggly Wiggly gigs to build ammo—*dollar
per box.* Sometimes Barbara cooks tea. Most times
she doesn't. Twice a year Hoyle takes it all down
to Mississippi, digs a hole, buries it. *Goin to the holes.*
No one knows *how many* or *where at.* I imagine
one big well: thousands of little brass hot-links,
puckered like a boil on Byhalia's neck. Did
my mother ever sit on the porch, squatting
by the blackfilled bowl? Coffee-spooning gun powder?
I've never touched a bullet. When my mother
tells me what they taste like, I wonder
what else that kind of girl knows.

Everyone Was Diagnosed with ADHD in the Nineties

I don't know the girl I was the four years
I overlapped with Hoyle: always boiling.
Picking beetles off a trailer cat. Stomp-scaring geese,
trying to yell the hot out my gut. We'd fish,
too, me weirdly still by the pond, shirtless
because he was. *Imagine a cantaloupe big as a belly.*
Imagine it's also a bomb, my mother says of little me,
my pulsing fits. *Imagine the only way to stop the bomb*
is to squeeze it tight and whisper. Or fish with granddad,
apparently. Me and Hoyle, pondwater quiet. I don't
know the girl patient enough for catfish, a hook sucked
into its cheek. I don't know the man beside her,
how he pacified my melon-meat. But I know how to dress
a fish. Screwdriven to a tree. Still glossed with pond.

Real Good Meat Eater

Screwed to a scaffold, body-water glossy,
the hog opens like a Bible. My mother
will not eat gizzard or liver, and I—   I admit—
resent a laborious chew. *You find a good stump*
and you whip the intestines round it 'til you
get out all the you-know-what, Hoyle says,
like the shit's what's scary and not
the sow pinned to the poplar, the man it took
to do it. Chop, boil, salt. Sup grateful the pluck.
I know. I try. Effortful with liver, tonguing the tongue.
It's work, getting inside, but in truth I never
saw it: the middle of June in Eads, Tennessee, the sun
evil-hot and physical, and Hoyle, sixty-five, back dark
as rhubarb, beating the absolute hell out of a tree
with a rope the body made.

The Butcher's Granddaughter

This body. Its rope. Before some pea-ball burst
his brain, I remember Hoyle's belly—me, curled
like a grub there, grogged on applesauce. He smelled
like a good lunch meat, the biggest man I knew, singing
too-ra-loo-ra-lai through a mouth I never heard bite.
Barbara, thin and brutal, delegated whipping to him. His
hands, which touched my brow like a thumb testing pith.
These guts predate us. My mother loved her father most,
tells me how much my walk echoes his. My heavy heel,
as unsubtle as Hoyle pacing on the hardwood. I could say
I am not of this viscous twine but here—it is. A borborygmi
beneath the hum, braided into her, braided into me.
Since birth. My mother's hot offal. Hoyle's
slain hog.

My Dad Has Sleep Apnea and Has a Gun
in His Nightstand

Once—I was a girl, at my dad's for the weekend—
the neighbor met my dog unkindly, which, by my metric,

meant he had to die. *Or*, said Mallory, a Catholic kid who
one time beat me with a Razor scooter, who showed me

the word *fingered* in her sister's diary. She nodded
at Mr. Edd's brand-new Mazda, nacreous as a clam's-hinge,

then pedaled us to the Circle K, where we bought all
the bologna our sports bras could carry. Original. Cheddar-

jalapeño. Sweetonion. This was summer. And *noon*.
What a reek was gathered as we mumped Edd's hood

with discs of flesh—unwell areolae of olive-flecked
ham—and how bold I must've been to wreck a man's

car and declare *someone's earned an Otter Pop*. So bold
I'd forgotten the sun, the treebare yard. Our neighborhood

of eyes. I'd forgotten my father, only a wall's-width
away. If he'd seen, he'd seen, but—we needed

to know, so we slunk up to his door. Heard nothing.
My dad, sometimes, made no sounds while sleeping, unable

to shift the bulging bridge in the choke-spot of his throat,
so we waited for the whale haul of breath, then crept in.

Mallory scrammed when she saw the Magnum in the drawer, but I
stayed, listening for breath in his body-near-drowned. Toeing

the coiled serpent of his CPAP machine. Crimped with my
new-and-keen meanness, I wondered . . . if I dragged him,

sharp by the arm from some breathless dream, would he—
then Edd, knuckling the storm door. My dog in a frantic

yammer. *Did you see anything? Anyone?* asked Edd, and dad
looked at me. Brows unreadable. Said, *I don't*, said, *I mean*, said,

I was home the whole time. And later, in the bathroom, I saw:
my mouth, rubied with juice.

Things Dying & Where

I.

M says the neighbor's house is burning and I
do not think but the rabbits but the cat I take
my macbook and shoes outside the heat
and conical reach of it like red-piked lupine we
have not got rain in weeks still I have not thought
but the rabbits but the cat I do not feel absolutely
a thing but my eyes hungry for the house's taking
the melting roof-glass the porch's fiber-optics its
kneeling joists will the house entire bow we wonder
will it crush the new fig tree my car our small
colony how shallow this worry while our neighbor
in the bluest t-shirt feebles sweat on the curb we
didn't lose a thing but sleep the rabbits   dumb with smoke.

II.

When the first litter dies I ask will you still
undress their bones and M halves a sandwich
which I share badly which becomes a beard of tomato-fat
he says no says what a little bit of skin this is coffins them
in compost we drink a can of something he says possum
or raccoon even his half-eared housecat might unbury them
but no measure we take can keep an animal out so we
drink a can of something the neighbor's house a black and
ruptured bellows the block a reek of cookout we drink a can
of something the problem is he says the mama rabbit
doesn't want to kindle when he reaches in she tears a cuss
in his hand her mouth red like fire like lupine and we
drink a can of something this town   has been strange to me.

Poem Written as Barter for $366.12 in Outstanding Bills

for Great Lakes Educational Loan Services, Inc.

All I want to win is the most laughs
and never die. All I want to grow
is the tongue that tricks
my neighbor, *no I have not took*

& burnt your siding to cook
my soups. I don't need anyone
except when I do. Except when I
pluck up too much from the road.

Elsewise only me sees the stump
with a pickaxed middle, the diner's
accumulated fry-oil, its guard of nurse-mean
wasps, the sun rubycut in the chrome

of a passing truck packed
with crushed chicken. I gather
like a glimmer-drunk bird, almost
believing I plume for plume's-

sake, but a grackle doesn't dance
for charity. It's just that I will not
raise bread for anyone but me. Or, no—
it is just that I will not think *yes okay*

about needing like air, needing like
I will not survive this river. I am a lot
of big trees. I am restless in bed. But—
listen, I'm not paying you

nothing. I can sing
about an acorn gourd.
The word *opaline*.
Bread in your mouth.

Dog Not Deer

me and my entire life stuck fast on I-40 between panting semis
and sedans bikes chattering like rat-jaws all of us filibustered in

the soy fields because some unseen gridlock couldn't wait until
the highway's third lane opens near Beebe to sit down I've taken off

my shoes in the reddening daylight a family stalls their van to stretch
to save a little gas the kids carousel away from the car kicking at

jigsaw glass and tire-rinds when they spot a shape scudded to pulp
on the shoulder a jammy pillowcase all fur and flies the bigger one's face

does a centrifugal pinch like a dumpling's peak-point and I mark
the boy's mouth *dog* he says *not deer* I don't know how he knows but

I imagine I do legible ear one unsullied leg I remember when I
was little our gentle wolfhound allowed whole hands in his mouth

but all my friends lillied when they saw him even Mallory bigger
than me who one time hucked her kneecap back into place while I

watched one day I stepped outside and saw the dog disarticulating
a squirrel who screamed me or the dying thing at his feet dog not deer

I touched his tongue he let me forty-five minutes or one mile later I see
the beached eighteen-wheeler that held us up blackened as catfish

in the median I don't have anyone to say *shit* to so I say *shit* out
the rolled-down window am beaten in the breath by something

creamier than exhaust what did I want it to be why is it worse to learn
dog not *deer* why did I read the child's mouth when I knew I didn't

want it named shouldn't I mourn everything that dies in the Delta
traffic thins I lose the van the ricefield flats fizz up into points of shale

shortleaf pine dark purpling the drive behind-my-belly is one end
of a bungee cord the other sunk in a stray's grave when Mallory

asked me what I wanted to be when I grew up I said
dog not deer dog not deer dog not deer

Self-Portrait as Haruno Sakura, Kunoichi of Konohagakure

I remember the first woman I hated—hair pink
as a sucked melon, knuckles bread-dough clean
under her chin. Her little knives. I hated her enough
to wish her dead (by ice! or opened-throat! whatever
so long as she's gone from the story)—but fear
is an easy-sleeved thing in a child. Hate a quick jacket.
She was a child, too—one who lived with me
in many bedrooms. A girl, growing, very much in love,
and early-spilling into the loose palm of a bra. Violent
in the way of twelves. Listen: this is who I wanted
to be. A woman who makes atomic the mace of her hands,
who pulps a man and howls in the doing. A woman
whose fist rubbles the bluff. A woman who bites the finger
from her forehead, saying through a mouthful of bone: *shannaro.*

Carne e Spirito

We need to be responsible carnivores.

—Dario Cecchini, Antica Macelleria Cecchini

I.

Twenty-three and listing, I find myself
behind a butcher's case, hoof squared
against my chest, and Aaron, thumbs loom-
looped in trotter, pulling.

It is hard   to take the skin off a thing.

I learn this as the pale sheet
unstitches, our fingers   like clockspring tools
carving slough from tender.
While Aaron bandsaws the naked wrist, I
tight-stretch the skin over flame,
lighting its sparse hairs in a quick stink.
Boil-then-bake. *Shatter*, says Aaron,
edgewards inwards. Makes bigger crackle.

II.

The first time I see the whole opened hog,
I think how the intestine unloads like a froth,
eager-packed in the widening split from groin
to rib. How like a palmful of blackberry, or
clouds of water-egg   crowding my hand.
Some we cut for tripe, some we plumb
for casing: thin, it seems, as a locust-wing,

45

and stored beside a catalogue
of cow heads in the freezer. Some pink-ripped
grins still gunked with cud. Claiming a skull
for souse, I cave a temple and find the cold moss
almost   sleepy. To think—
this quiet mass once fed four stomachs.

III.

Bold enough to boil aspic, to shuck silverskin
from deckle, I think I can   manage   slaughter.
The order in which you end an animal is not
the order of lessons learned.

I buy a rabbit fat with milk, her litter
still bean-clung to her belly, and this I grow
in my own backyard: a dozen quickening bodies.

First, I learn, a noon-gutting means flies.
Second: it stares back because it dies before its brain
can say *close*. Third: alfalfa distracts.
Fourth: place the broom across its neck
while it eats. Fifth: stand on the broom, find
its legs like wheelbarrow grips. Sixth: haul.

IV.

When I tell Aaron *I'm writing a poem about butchery*
he says *again* and also *headcheese, petite tender,*
spider, secreto. The first rabbit I slaughtered
I didn't. I pulled and felt pops one-two-three, the cervical
vertebrae spreading like wings (instant death,
the internet told me). And she stared, quiet, as I nailed her feet
to a tree. Barely wasting blood.

Froth. Egg. Then I slipped the gut-hook in her belly
and   she screamed.

Became My Body, Too

I.

when from the river my mother came and made me of the river
I drug myself out from the river and together we made   the river

two long dorsals of eyelash-and-bone our skin still a screen into the aquarium

    of us

       I said   *how much of us will make this world*
       she said   *as many eyes as there are hawk moths*
                    as many stomachaches as there are good fires

and being of the river I said *what is a fire*   so she said

baby   *go as far from me as you can*

       and comb your hair with a jaw you didn't

               ask to open

II.

I was lucky.   I got to grow up slow.

Mitzi, at twelve, could make anything gravy
while her mother, Barbara,   slim as a bulrush,

chewed through a mouth of boiled Pepsi: *pick it up pick it up pick it up*

                                                    dumbass

(when I tell my mother I like to write   she says, pleased,
        so did your grandmother).

At night, Mitzi would kneel by her sister's bunk
with a garden-trowel   the grip all gnawed,
(*how can a mouth   so small   blister beechwood?*)—watching
for the pulse of jaw,   the frenetic socket-whirl
that took the girl's body
before she became crack of cymbal   and seafloor lightning.

She knew how to worm gunpowder smudge

from her father's   dark sleeves

(once she set the cycle too hot,
        knocked out the navy with the powdermeal;

her sister said   *daddy's gonna beat you 'til you cain't grow no more*).

49

For seven years, Mitzi owned a single bra.
I imagine the bleached elastic   an angry diagram
    against my mother's unbuttered ribs—
      she never broke a hundred
        until me.

III.

Of men, my mother says   *they will touch you.*
Of men, my mother says   *you're just too   damn   little*
                            for your own good.

Of men—the first husband hauled her eighteen-year-old bones and
    her yellow-and-steel guitar and her two new bras to the Grand
    Canyon, where they
smoked weed until   —my mother says   *baby,*

find you a man   *who don't think like you do.*

IV.

Barbara comes up from the river,   drenched in coontail kelp
   and fresh-mussel,

        pale   as a goat throat,

and she says   *Hi darlin'.*
I say   *Hi, Barbara.*
She says   *How's your mama?*
I say   *Not great, Barbara.*   (Here, Barbara
                                    lights a cigarette.)

I ask if all ghosts smoke cigarettes, like, is that a thing.
Uh-uh, says Barbara, and, *Don't you start, baby.*
I tell her I won't.

V.

Anyway, Barbara says, *I hear you got this poem. I just,   I wanna,
look—*

once, her sister seized at the Kroger   between Jiffy-bread
and Bisquick and my mother in a panic   put all ten
fingers in her sister's mouth and held there, didn't make a sound,
didn't cry as her baby   sister near bit off both thumbs

(my mother told me there was a way sis smelled   after
a seizure   right on the top of her head: like the
deepest place of sand, like a dinosaur's footprint)

—you got to know we weren't all that mean.

VI.

"... Make no mistake. As a child, if you screwed up, your
body wore it for a while. But it was a different time. Mom,
though she could present like a pissed off silverback, had
deep wounds I never understood or saw 'til I was grown. She
was very wounded and very loving and soft, trying to hide
herself in her own adult-found strength. Which by the way
was all hers. She earned it and let that bleed onto me.

As a child I loved her. AS A TEEN I HATED HER. As an
eventual equal I loved her the most cause I understood. Oh
God how much she would love you. Big, deep, honestly, with
a fullness of a personal cheerleader. She ADORED you. You
were perfect. She had a near photographic memory. If she
read it once, she always knew it. Her sister Jimmy Lou had
a better memory."

VII.

My friends and I joke
that if we ever get shoved in some   dirty old car,
it'll be my mother breathing fire, just   tearing into the guy,
                                             saying, *it's alright, baby. It's alright.*

I think she could pull a bear in half.

Lonnie, her Lonnie, he can't help   the choke of his swollen liver.
He can't   reach his toes anymore, so my mother cuts   what grows,
and he grows   tumors and angrier. He can't help it.   Or her.

I watch, one day, as she takes the 2 qt. Pyrex out to the yard. It's November—
air still thick with bradford—

and I know she's going to drop it and I know it's going to break, so I watch,
instead, my mother's face   become soda-glue, become belt welt,
become dogwood and clumped muscadine, become tea, become wooden
spoon, become ten fingers, become nacre, become a well so deep.

VIII.

My mother says when rent was short   and Barbara was lithium-
       sick, her father would walk   to the pool hall.

    What he made was: ends meet.

         (but sometimes he came back with a paper boat
         of four cold chicken strips—salted and big with
         batter—for my mother whose sleep, he knew,
         was light.)

         (in the unlit kitchen. teeth breaching.
            she says, *you would not believe*   *this chicken.*)

I own   but cannot use   his custom pool-cue.

Rock maple. My height.

IX.

"You consider the shades of things. She was more black and
white. Dad was a rainbow. Beautiful, colorful. Would admit
and apologize lovingly full wrongness. Sometimes tearfully.
He felt so deeply. Mom was defensive. Her wounds were
never healed. She could not forgive.

I made a choice not to be them on the surface and raised
you differently but you grew from their genes and much
of them you still are. And I adore you."

X.

The first time,   she did not   say

    my body is a beanpod, mysteriously zippered.

What she said, instead: *I hate this man. I will not keep*   *his*
    evidence, and

        for many years the soil held no shoots.

        I do not hate to be called miraculous.

XI.

When I call my mother after making myself

                                                abruptly single,

        she says, *well   you can't give a man*
        what you won't even give your mama, and though

she is speaking of phone-calls,   I am frightened by this girth of self.

As though I was extracted with it. How much am I loveless and how
    much does it matter.

Just wait, she says,   *'til you have a baby of your own.*

        Later, corn-bald—I wonder me in the mirror:

                my foot's crooked edge
                the drunken opals of my knees
                each convexed, unfuckwithable thigh
                my face   my lovely
                                brick fist of a face

                and deeper, the wet soft wall   that thickens
                then gives   like some mean goose.

        Gentle,   gutty ruckus.

My mother was made aware of me at thirty-six,   had already,
I think, surrendered   to the notion of never-being-mother.

I imagine her   in wake of this news, also
examining her body.

                              Her stomach's new nacre.

I do not want a baby.

Not even the down what builds it.

Poem Written as Barter for $75.00 in Outstanding Bills

for LabCorp

I whittle mud from my boot like anyone else.
I pluck hair from my chin.
I like to have a party
where everyone's dressed good.

Listen, we will disagree on some
things, like paper waste, and tact, and
some people need a reminder, and a few people
need more than just one reminder, and no people

sit at the door all day dog-slobbering
for an envelope from Decherd County's
only goddamn urgent care, but wait—wait.
I know. I do owe. This far from the river

I am not often told take care
or pay your doctor, so of course
you find me here, eating unwashed
things—strawberry, apple-skin. I think

a tooth can handle that, though I night-
mare mine crumbling like feta
in my palm. I am still new this, to caring
for bodily me, which is not to say I need

to be loved. Except I do. The clinic
was neat, the nurse easy with my wine-burnt
throatback. Her finger dug in my underjaw
was the first time I'd been touched

in months. You can't know
how many minutes I spent on this. For you.
What's a dollar when I'm telling you
I trembled like a bathing animal.

Lineage

what spills from your lips into your palm / —blood puddled—
    —Ángel García

I sleep my teeth
out of me—always
in pieces. Shattered
like a booted ice cube.
In these dreams, I am
a little bit convinced
This Is Fine. The second
tooth-losing. *Now I will get*
my bigger jaw for chewing
my bigger meats, as though
every mouth gets a legacy
of bones. Drinking Sprites
with a newly pregnant friend,
I say: lately I've been
extremely aware what
occupies me, but I don't
actually—actually, I say: the ceiling
fell in at my dad's house
because too many roof-
rats made a toilet of the attic.
I imagine my mouth
soused with critters.
Jittering whatever truss
seems wanting. I read
dental fixation indicates
a number of things—*teeth*
falling out means embarrassment

teeth falling out means power-
lessness teeth falling out means
money teeth falling out
means—but I don't need
teeth to tell me I'm
afraid my whole family
doesn't know me
because I made me
that way. In my dreams,
sometimes I coax
the pieces. Like glass
from a foot. Eggshard
from omelet. Bramble-
root from soil, if soil
was gums.

Things Dying & Where

It seems my father has been old
an awfully long time. It's likely
he will die that way. *Funny grapes*,
he calls the Minnehaha choke-
cherry, cuffing the bunch. *Itty-bitty*.

What a bear-weird shape, my father,
in the hale grey of this place. Eyes
souped & wild. He smells of a tired
mustard. Everything seems ready
to take him: the lichen, the falls,
the hungry earth. When he trips
I don't catch him, because I am small, I say,
or because he is darkened & peltlike,
nape loose as a great-backed animal
& gravied with sweat. The late
bloom of him.

Oop, he says.
Sorry, honey, & stands, brushing the veinless
space under his knee. My father's lessening
is a strange harvest: each fingertip
a skulk of borzoi, his nose a waxy
Spanish lamppost, his eyes an ink-
pewter & baby's dough. When he falls
I don't catch him,

his fiddled-with heart
already the rhododendron root-ball.

Tennessee Wildman

This Wildman approached women with "wild, horrid screams"
while attempting to carry them off. He was described as tall, with
great muscular strength and covered in dark matted hair. He also
ran with swiftness that "defied both men and dogs."

—Ashley Radar, for the *Elizabeth Star*

I.

The bar is a lake of baseball caps, a dozen
gold-trimmed—Korea. Vietnam. The goin-out

caps—when he walks in, young and jacket-wrapped
despite July licking the bricks outside,

every stool-hunched legionnaire sits straight,
sloughed cheeks plumping. Earl leans in:

them lashes dark and hearty as some horse legs.
Emory says, *I'll be,* and *what kinda man orders Coke*

and a decaf. The stranger pulls bills from his pocket,
loose and dewy as tissue-packing. Looks

at the sign next to the age-murked clock
overhead: NO DOPE SMOKEN, NO CURSIN,

NO FREE LODEN. What happens next
plumbs the descriptive capacity of all

fifteen drunk veterans and Abigail Palisade,
the weekend bartender. He's there, and then

he's not.

II.

Coaxed by a rare week of breeze
to the pedestrian bridge, two kids point

at a big blue hunch across the river, something
pimpling the woods there, and behind them

he sits, also looking—broad as a sail-yard,
poorly shirted. Abigail has never seen someone stay

so still. Skin supernaturally dry. By each bench-
leg, clockwise: a spuming anthill, one pearly

and naked can, his boot, his other boot. He sees her,
pats a slim wedge of sitting space by his leg.

One of the kids shouts *TRUCK*. On the far bank,
the blue: a Ford bed, axed by earth, like the

clean-sucked jaw of some lousy possum.

III.

The morning still clogged and light-
hungry, Abigail invites him in for aeropress

and half a biscuit. He was only meant
to pass through, he says, on a drive—but

he remembered being very young and here
with his family, eating a catfish poboy

so stunning he thought it a dream-sandwich
until *ten minutes ago when I recognized*

the smell of the ditch-creek behind your house,
and, so dulled with hunger *and having known*

the perfect sandwich, I didn't see it, the rotting tree,
primed for collapse beside the mailbox.

He finishes the biscuit. Neglects the coffee.
Abigail's chair makes a sound like a goat. *Well.*

Gettin to be that time.

IV.

He doesn't return next week, or the next.
Emory's back to curdling his coffee with

rum he thinks Abigail won't snatch, and she's
corkscrewing rags so hard she splits a snifter

like a pecan. How does a ditch smell? How
doesn't she know. When the landlady cleared

the totaled tree from her driveway, she asked,
It rain recently? Gotta be lightning what did

this. Abigail tries to remember the make
of his car, the color of his jacket, but all she tastes

is the roof of her mouth and mud.

V.

Shift-swapped, Abigail spends her Friday
dunking sheets of meat in cornmeal, salt,

paprika, black pepper. Milk, yolk, repeat. She
spoons these into oil, tender as an empty egg

in dye, and watches each fillet gold like a fat
summer moon. She beds them all in too much slaw.

A days-old French roll. She fries more fish
than she could eat in a week, then fries more, and

when she runs out of bread she hunts other pockets:
books, opened-up envelopes, two hearty fern fronds,

her hands. Next, she plates. Thirteen. Eighteen.
Twenty-five poboys in total, soft with remoulade

and jellied tomato. She saddles it all on a
buckling plant caddy, wheels it to the back door.

The plates cattle all the way to the ditch,
where she finds him. Waiting. She slides

down the bank.

Fox Song

Clung up in the Cumberland Plateau
we do our best at no-sleep-needing.

Hoverfly unperturbable. We
miracle the porch—reading

poems. Eating whiskey. A friend
said she saw a fox here,

hoped the same for me.
In four days I have seen

every living skink. Seen,
also, a man's very full

short-leg. I love the look
of that. A door of any make

at capacity. I wonder.
How me might fit there.

Night here a good
thin blanket and breathable.

Are you sure, I narrow-eye the stars,
the spuddy half-moon, *you did not*

knit this for me. But the reservoir
is deep, and the reservoir is

deep. The bed not mine. I cannot
touch that thigh. Do you remember

the lake? How we couldn't see
no one in the dark. Just two dozen

bodies. Voice. I wasn't there, but
given the lightlessness

I could say I was.

Self-Portrait as Lin, Who Knows the Bathhouse

Name one no-name woman, one no-mother tub-scrubber, who
can pluck as I the packed mussels of soap from a bath wall; name one

whose pantknees turn as black as mine by night, as pink by dawn.
When I paused my drudge for a little human hand,

I didn't call it *love*—I thought, only, here lies another
new board for the floor, another rag for waxing. Not here is

my inarticulate sister, made newly nameless. Not here is her track
of vertebrae rising from a fat baby back, like the sea-sunk railroad after rain.

To sleep in a comb of working women is to know a lot of knuckles, restless arms
flung from sleep-deep bodies. I haven't dreamt a day. (But. Maybe. Maybe

there's a dreaming only bodies do.) So when the foreman pushed her
towards the Big Tub, I did what a dirtyknees does: I kneeled,

I said *I'm coming to get you, I won't let him hurt you*, as, maybe,
I or other no-name no-dreams have been hurt. And I buffed the tub.

Calling up, from a deep boiling place, salt and rose-petal, citrus pulp
and powdered soda. I was here before her and I am here after, pearling

candy for the soot-which-breathes. I was here before and I am here after.
So when she slips the knot at the Big Tub, I reach my hands alongside her.

I wind. We have a rich guest. *We have a rich guest.*
Stay right where you are. I'm coming to get you.

Discourse

for Mary Oliver

What I want to say is what
I want to say. I ran the water

poach-hot, watched my shoulder
rose like a struck cheek. Because

something there. Unwinds. In the
way water slucks. In seventh grade,

the first-chair trumpet never
looked at me and I loved him.

I put my foot through a wall. I didn't
want anyone. To know. Me, peach-

softening in the bleachers. Me, lush
as a honey-sick ermine. I nearly

bit my mom in half. How'd I get me
into this? Saying palm-puddled

daisyleaf in place of *sorry*. It's not
like shattered drywall is some easier

words—because I had to caulk it all back
myself. It's maybe that I won't believe

words lack feet. And fur. I'm not in this
to be misunderstood, though I was.

Before. Distracting with a wrecked beanfield,
or gargled-up okra stuff—but now

I mean it when I say I'm willful
as yogurt in the sunshine. How it's

made slow cheese. Look, I wrote a poem
to tell you something genuine. Though.

It doesn't always seem that way. I still
believe folding a fisheye in lardo and salt

is the best way for you to feel the dream
that sucked sleep out of me. So. I sit down

with the green of many slick frogs. The sharp
and insufficient air of a mountainside.

The eatable gouda rind. What I think
was a buck last night, groaning like a ship.

Butterflies Are More Metal than Moths

> *We here present the results of [male butterflies] only, because it*
> *was difficult to obtain enough number of females for the study.*
> —Chen et al, *Frontiers in Ecology and Evolution*

a common bluebottle sees five times

                    the colors we manage

what I imagine here

                    cannot be imagined

which leads me to wonder

                    what's a ruddy hunk of marigold to

a butterfly's eye

                    citrus-fractal, gunk for bees, or

does the bud weird speech

                    like a mouth plumbed inside out

I guess what I'm asking is

                    can butterflies see ghosts and if so

how many have I watered in a jar

                    how many butterflies have laughed at me for

fingering a ghost's nose or sometimes

                    gummily sucking a chicken bone in the yard

because I think no one sees me

                    elbows propped on a rotten patio-beam

save the moths licking lamplight

                                  beige and cabbagey

lingering in the night's hot-damp

                                  I thought myself a moth

because I can bonk at bright things

                                  a real long time

then I read some moths are born

                              mouthless but this doesn't work

for me, starving and moon-beautiful

                              because I'll drink any color

especially what's invisible

                              when a swallowtail wants wet

it finds what it can

                              puddling mud rot occasionally

blood's slick gel

                              red seeping blue seeping black

J. Bailey Hutchinson Moves 658.8 Miles North and Tries to Make It Count

Here I go to hot-eye the road. To waller dirt like a sun-hungry
centipede. Because. This warm licks different. What do I say about
this town except it's not mine, never made me, and that's okay? To
count the staples in a pole and not know them. To smell the river
un-rouxed. Saturn, protein, the way my stepdad jaundiced in his
recliner—who knows why I won't sit still, but here I go to cow your
arm, tongue wide as a shoebox. I don't know who to be anymore,
but I wonder the me that wine sicked every Ozark Tuesday, and
Thursday, and Sunday, fourthplacing my mother who lives alone
and is dying of it. Once, night-buttered, I rode my bike down a
hill and begged that something might unexist me. Here I go to get
grateful nothing did. The lakes, new and rootsunk, remind me what
I haven't held on to, and I want to ask, *who told you? Who dumped all
my no-goods*—like you aren't what moments every water? Despite,
I call up my mother—we speak good. Bird-fluent. She is generous.
The sun over the river is bladder colored. The sun in the low
mountain blanched. Here, I watch the sun with a doglike *almost*,
thinking: I am so nearly doomed, but there is a woman I might be.

"Self-Portrait as Tomoe Mami, Beheaded by a Witch" references the anime *Puella Magi Madoka Magica*. In the series, a catlike creature named Kyubey approaches middle school girls and offers to grant them any wish if they agree to take on magical powers and fight evil creatures known as "witches." The *magical girl* subgenre is arguably one of the most recognizable types of anime (*Sailor Moon* being the most famous example); these narratives often address concepts such as hope, friendship, love, purity of heart, and other traditionally "feminine" themes. In *Madoka Magica*, the character initially framed as the protagonist's mentor (Tomoe Mami) is brutally beheaded by a witch in the third episode—a violent departure from the genre's standard tropes.

The form for **"J. Bailey Hutchinson Takes Plan B in Marseille"** comes from Christian Anton Gerard, whose poem "Christian Anton Gerard Moving Toward Psalm" uses the same self-naming refrain.

"Self-Portrait as Haruno Sakura, Kunoichi of Konohagakure" references the anime *Naruto*, which follows a generation of kids training to become highly skilled shinobi. Sakura is a member of the central group of shinobi-in-training, and during her early arc she's fueled almost entirely by her infatuation with her teammate Sasuke. Sakura later grows into a physically gifted warrior capable of shattering mountains with a single punch, but as a preteen I hated her character. I found her boring and frustrating; I thought she was stupid for pining after Sasuke. When I got older, I realized I didn't hate Sakura at all—I hated that the series author accredited all her strength to her love for Sasuke rather than letting her be powerful for her own sake. (Oh, and Sakura also often yells "shannaro," or "dammit," when she punches things.)

"Carne e Spirito" borrows its title from a presentation by master Italian butcher Dario Cecchini. Cecchini argues for a "responsible" form of carnivorism that ensures a safe and pleasant life for the animals we eat, encourages the use of the whole carcass, and honors the gift of an animal's body. He posits that butchery is an art not unlike poetry, so long as it's done benevolently with a humble heart and compassion for all living things. As he talks during the titular presentation, he's also eviscerating a hog.

"**Became My Body, Too**" includes two Facebook messages lifted directly from my mother. It's important to me that she has a voice in this manuscript—aside from the poetic voice I've concocted for her.

"**Self-Portrait as Lin, Who Knows the Bathhouse**" references the Studio Ghibli film *Spirited Away*. Lin is a longtime resident and employee of a spirits-only bathhouse run by the witch Yubaba; she takes Chihiro, the movie's protagonist, under her wing after Chihiro pledges to work at the bathhouse to free her parents from a spell that turned them into pigs. Lin helps her begrudgingly at first but quickly grows quite fond and protective of Chihiro.

"**Tennessee Wildman**" is a loose retelling of Tennessee's very own Sasquatch myth.